DIY Succulents

DIY Succulents

From Placecards to Wreaths,
35+ Ideas for Creative Projects with Succulents

Tawni Daigle

Avon, Massachusetts

Published by
Adams Media, a division of F+W Media, Inc.
57 Littlefield Street, Avon, MA 02322. U.S.A.
www.adamsmedia.com

ISBN 10: 1-4405-8808-2
ISBN 13: 978-1-4405-8808-2
eISBN 10: 1-4405-8809-0
eISBN 13: 978-1-4405-8809-9

Printed in the United States of America.

10 9 8 7 6 5 4 3 2 1

Library of Congress Cataloging-in-Publication Data
Daigle, Tawni.
    DIY succulents / Tawni Daigle.
        pages cm
    Includes index.
    ISBN 978-1-4405-8808-2 (pb) -- ISBN 1-4405-8808-2 (pb) -- ISBN 978-1-4405-8809-9 (ebook)
-- ISBN 1-4405-8809-0 (ebook)
    1. Succulent plants. 2. House plants in interior decoration. 3. Container gardening--Equipment
and supplies. I. Title.
    SB438.D25 2015
    635.9'525--dc23

2015015389

Cover design by Frank Rivera.
Photography by Tawni Daigle.

This book is available at quantity discounts for bulk purchases.
For information, please call 1-800-289-0963.

Dedication

To my mom and dad for all of the sacrifices they have made and for always encouraging me to follow my dreams . . .

To my husband for loving me unconditionally and supporting me in doing what I love . . .

And to my precious children Brodie, Bailen, Avrie, and Bastian, for giving me purpose and inspiring me to live every day intentionally.

Contents

Chapter 4: In the Garden 95

Chapter 5: Succulent Accessories 141

Chapter 6: Succulent Holidays 159

Chapter 7: Celebrating with Succulents 179

Index 199

Acknowledgments

Looking back, I am so grateful for all of the people who helped make this book possible. With three rowdy kids and an infant, writing a DIY book was no easy task. Thankfully, I've got quite the support team, without which I'd still be on page one.

First of all, thank you to Christine Dore and everyone at Adams Media who believed in me and thought I would be a good fit for writing this book. A huge thank you to my editor, Laura Daly, for all of your feedback and guidance.

To my dearest friend, Krista Mares: It would have been literally impossible for me to write this book without your help. Your creativity and energy were a driving force behind every project and your help with the kids was invaluable. Thank you for encouraging me to start *Needles + Leaves*, and for always being there.

To my husband, Spike: Words cannot express how thankful I am for you. You believed I could do this, and your support and encouragement helped make it happen. Thank you for letting me go crazy at the craft and hardware stores, and for not minding when I spent way too much time at the nursery picking out the perfect plants. Thank you for urging me to pursue my passions, and for working hard so that I can do the things I love.

To my littles, Brodie, Bailen, Avrie, and Bastian: Thank you for being patient with me over the past few months while we were all waist deep in succulents. You four make me laugh and help me keep the important things in life in perspective. I love you all more than you will ever know.

To my parents, Chris and Marci Mares: I owe so much to you both. Thank you for praying for me and always letting me be myself. Thank you for the many sacrifices you have made over the years and for being by my side supporting me no matter what my endeavor. Mom, thank you for passing down your "green thumb" and for always giving me advice when I need it.

To my amazing in-laws, Mike and Caroline Daigle: Thank you for offering to hang out with the kids so I could escape to write for a few hours here and there. Most of this book was written in those coffee shop sessions, so thank you for making yourselves available and for your willingness to help make this book happen.

Thank you so much to Karen Hana and everyone at Rancho Vista Nursery for providing so many gorgeous plants for this book. Thank you for your kindness and for sharing your extensive knowledge.

Thank you to Peter Loyola, of the Succulent Cafe Oceanside, for always inspiring me with your gorgeous arrangements. Your innovative succulent masterpieces have been a huge influence on the way I arrange my own plants.

Thank you to everyone who has read my blog or followed along on Instagram. Your "likes" and positive comments keep me motivated and always striving to improve. I absolutely love seeing your plant "babies" and hearing your success stories!

Lastly, thank you to my heavenly Father for creating this beautiful earth for us to enjoy and for instilling in me a passion and enthusiasm caring for and growing these amazing plants.

Introduction

FROM YOUR LOCAL COFFEE SHOP to department store windows, succulents seem to be making an appearance everywhere lately. Their stunning colors, geometric shapes, and resilience make them appealing to everyone, including those who don't consider themselves as having a "green thumb." Succulents are flourishing beyond your garden and are taking center stage as the go-to plant for weddings, gifts, crafting, home decor, and much more! If you're looking for dozens of ideas on how to use these amazing plants in a variety of areas of your life, this book is for you.

I received my very first succulent plant as a Mother's Day gift from my sister-in-law. It was a lovely green echeveria in a terra cotta pot she had painted turquoise. She used chalkboard paint to create a spot on the pot where she chalked in a little heart. It was adorable and I loved it dearly. Summer quickly approached and I thought my new plant would just love it out in the hot sun. After all, succulents grow in the desert, right? I decided to place it in direct sunlight in the midsummer heat.

Unfortunately, I hadn't done my homework on caring for succulents. Before long, the poor thing was scorched beyond recognition. It was done for. As I was about to throw it away, I spotted a tiny baby plant growing on the stem under the shriveled leaves. I didn't know anything about succulent propagation, but I pulled off the small pup and planted it. I was totally amazed when it started growing roots and flourishing all on its own! This is when I realized how incredible succulent plants are, and since then I've fallen in love with caring for them and watching them grow and multiply.

I was so fascinated by succulent propagation that I wrote my first blog post on the topic, not knowing if anyone else even cared about the subject. I started my blog *Needles + Leaves* (*www.needlesandleaves.net*) with my sister-in-law, Krista Mares, as a way to combine her passion for crafting and my love of succulents and photography. It's the perfect outlet for us. To my surprise, hundreds of thousands of people each year come to our blog to find out how to propagate and craft with their plants. It's so awesome to be able to share the knowledge I have gained with succulent lovers all over the world.

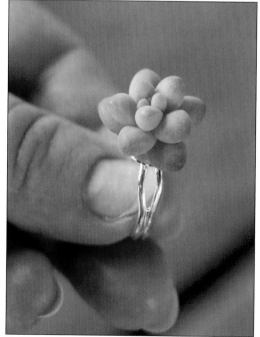

This book is divided into two parts. Part 1 is an introduction to caring for succulent plants. We will discuss common varieties of succulents, where to purchase them, how to pot them, the three essentials to growing healthy succulents, as well as how to propagate succulents from cuttings and leaves. Most of the projects in this book are considered "living art"; therefore, you should know how to care for and maintain the plants as they grow over time. Succulent propagation is very useful when you need many plants, especially small "babies," for a variety of projects.

Part 2 of this book is divided into five chapters: For the Home, In the Garden, Succulent Accessories, Succulent Holidays, and Celebrating with Succulents. Some of our projects will be simple, such as planting succulents in teacups, while others will be more involved (think power tools!). Don't worry, though—even beginners can tackle the more difficult projects.

Whether you're new to the world of succulents or have enjoyed them in your home for years, this book will provide information and inspiration to take your plants to the next level. Feel free to take my ideas and make them your own by using different plants or adding your own personal touches. Are you ready to get your hands dirty? Let's dig in!

Part 1

GETTING
STARTED

Chapter 1

Succulents 101

Succulents are rising in popularity, and with good reason. Their beauty and resilience make them perfect for creating tasteful, sophisticated, long-lasting works of living art. Although succulents have a reputation for being impossible to kill, there are some basic guidelines you should follow to keep your plants healthy and looking their best. In this chapter, you'll learn about some of the most common types of succulents and how to care for them.

What Is a Succulent?

Succulents are plants that have thick leaves, stems, or roots that store water in order to survive extended periods of drought. Their leaves and stems are often called "juicy" because they are capable of holding a lot of liquid in them.

Although they are commonly thought of as desert-dwelling plants, succulents are actually grown all over the world in many different climates. They have become a very popular houseplant in recent years because of their reputation for low maintenance. Their durability and ability to propagate easily make them the ideal plant for use in crafting and the types of arrangements we will create in this book. They come in many different colors, shapes, and sizes, so there will always be a succulent perfect for your project.

Succulent Cafe in Oceanside, CA

Common Varieties of Succulents

There are thousands of varieties of succulents available today. You might be overwhelmed when you see the number of options available at your local garden center, but the following breakdown will help you zero in on what variety is best for your needs.

ECHEVERIA

Echeverias are gorgeous rosette-forming plants that come in a variety of shapes and colors. From pointy to round, curly to ruffled, their leaves provide an endless array of geometric beauty. Best suited for USDA hardiness zones 8–11, their leaf colors can intensify with colder or warmer temperatures throughout the year. (To find your growing zone, visit *http://planthardiness.ars.usda.gov/PHZMWeb/*.) They range in diameter from 1" to 20". Some echeverias reproduce on their own by shooting off pups, which can be wiggled off and replanted. Echeverias have shallow roots, so they will do well in containers lacking depth.

GRAPTOPETALUM

Like echeverias, graptopetalums are rosette-forming succulents. They have thick leaves that can change color depending on the amount of sun exposure they receive. For example, *Graptopetalum paraguayense*, when placed in full sun, can appear bleached out, pink, orange, and even white—while the same plant kept in the shade might be a darker bluish gray with opalescent tips hinted with purple. Graptopetalums should be handled with care, as their leaves snap off quite easily. Over time, they tend to grow long stems as their lower leaves wither and fall off and new growth develops from the center of the rosette. They will grow very long and cascade unless you cut them off and replant them. Graptopetalums will do best in USDA hardiness zones 7–11.

SEDUM

There are many different types of sedum, from low-growing ground cover to varieties like *Sedum morganianum* (also called Burro's Tail) that cascade more than 3 feet. Many varieties are topped with starry flowers in summer and fall. Some members of the sedum family are commonly called stone-crop. They do best in USDA hardiness zones 3–9.

SEMPERVIVUM

Sempervivums are often referred to as "hens and chicks" because of their ability to reproduce by the sending of offsets. The offsets, or "chicks," are attached by an umbilical-like cord that can be cut and then the chick can be planted on its own. Sempervivums may be the most frost tolerant of all succulents, so if you need a cold-hardy plant, these are hardy in USDA zones 4–10. Sempervivums grow in rosettes and come in hundreds of varieties.

Sedum

Sempervivum

AEONIUM

Aeoniums are rosette-forming succulents that usually grow on a long, bare stem. They are not frost tolerant and do best in USDA zones 9–11. Purple aeoniums can tolerate full sun, while the green ones prefer some shade. Aeonium flowers come out of the center of the rosette, and in most cases the plant will die once it has set seed.

CRASSULA OVATA

Crassula ovata, commonly referred to as jade plant, is an evergreen that grows green leaves in pairs along thick stems. Some leaves may appear yellowish green or even reddish on the edges when exposed to lots of sunlight. Jade plants flower in winter or early spring. Jade plants are hardy in USDA zones 9–11.

Aeonium

Crassula ovata

CACTUS

Cacti are spiny plants that are typically found in very dry, desert-like environments. Cactus spines are modified leaves that defend against herbivores and provide limited shade. Cactus spines grow from areoles, which also give rise to flowers. Cacti are available in a variety of sizes ranging from only 1 cm to an enormous 63'.

TILLANDSIA (Also Called Air Plants)

Air plants get their name because they normally grow without soil while attached to other plants, gathering nutrients and moisture through the air. Using their roots as anchors, they absorb nutrients through their leaves. Thinner-leafed varieties tend to require more water, while those with thicker leaves can better tolerate drought. Tillandsia may bloom on a regular basis. They do best in USDA hardiness zones 9–11.

Cactus

Tillandsia (Also called air plants)

Rancho Vista Cactus and Succulent Nursery in Vista, California.

How and Where to Buy Succulents

The great news: Succulents are readily available. From your local big-box garden centers to grocery stores and farmers' markets, you don't have to look far to find them.

If you are looking for quality and variety, you may want to check out a local nursery. Some nurseries sell directly to the public, and if you can cut out the middleman, you are likely to take home healthier plants. You're likely to pay around $2 to $5 for a smaller plant and up to $20 for a larger one.

When purchasing succulents, it's important to make sure they are free from pests and diseases. Check the center of your plant and under its leaves for aphids and mealybugs (see a later section for more information). Make sure the leaves are not soggy or black, which are signs of rot.

Succulents can also be purchased online if necessary, but it's always good to see them in person whenever possible before buying.

Succulents Alongside Children and Pets

There are a few succulent plants that can be poisonous if ingested. You can avoid this problem altogether by hanging your plants or keeping them out of reach of your children and pets. Cats often chew on plants to get chlorophyll to aid their digestion. It's a good idea to keep barley grass available for your cats to chew instead of your succulents. Kalanchoes, Euphorbias, and Agaves are on the list of potentially harmful succulents.

The Best Pots for Succulents

Succulents thrive when grown in containers, especially well-draining terra cotta, concrete, and stone pots. Most succulents have shallow root systems, so shallow, wide pots are perfect for creating a home for your plants. In most cases, deep pots are a waste of soil and the soil takes longer to dry out. Since succulents suffer if their roots sit in soggy soil, it's important to choose containers with drainage holes.

In this book, the variety of containers used may require some alterations to create good drainage systems. For example, when you use a container with no drainage hole, you can drill one if possible, or create a soil-draining system with pebbles and/or moss. Any pebbles will do, as long as you are able to create a space for water to escape from the soil. You can also use long-fibered sphagnum moss in containers without drainage, because it absorbs a lot of water and then dries out quickly. This moss is great for succulents because they can get the water they need without suffering the damaging effects of sitting in excess water.

In a natural setting, succulents seem to do best when neglected. They are often found growing in the most unlikely places: in rock gardens, on walls, and in nooks and crannies between pavers, just to name a few.

Caring for Your Succulents

Just as with any other plant, there are three main factors to consider when growing succulents: soil, water, and sunlight. Using the correct type and amount of each of these factors will help your plants look their best.

SOIL

Succulents thrive in well-draining soil. You can buy bags of soil mixed especially for succulents and cacti at your local garden center. Kellogg Garden Organics Palm, Cactus & Citrus mix is one great option. Sometimes these store-bought mixes can contain undesirable sticks and such that can be sifted out if necessary. (For example, if you are making a tiny terrarium, big sticks might take up too much space.)

If you can't find specialized soil or if you have regular potting soil on hand that you'd rather use, you can customize it to best suit your succulent. To increase drainage, mix in equal parts:

- Regular potting soil
- Perlite (an expanded volcanic glass used to improve aeration and drainage) and/or
- Coarse-grained horticultural-grade sand

You can find both perlite and horticultural sand at garden centers. Succulents will suffer if their roots sit in excessive water, so it's worth the time up front to create a very well-draining soil.

Repot your succulents in fresh soil once a year to keep them healthy and looking their best.

WATER

There is a common misconception that succulents don't need much water. While it's true that they can go longer periods of time without it, they will not thrive in a drought-like situation. My general rule of thumb is to water your plants when the soil is completely dry—typically once a week during hotter months and a little less often when the weather cools. You can kill succulents by overwatering, so make sure the soil is totally dry between waterings.

To actually water the plants, give the soil a good soak so that the water runs out of the bottom of the pot. Try to water the *soil*, not the *plant*, if possible. Letting water settle on the leaves can cause rot, in addition to leaving unsightly markings.

If the pot you're using doesn't have drainage holes, don't soak the soil. Instead, give it more of a "sip." In this book, we will be creating arrangements in containers without drainage holes, such as teacups, Mason jars, and glass terrariums. Because succulents do better in containers that drain well, we will always layer the bottom of the container with pebbles to create an alternative drainage system. Although this isn't the ideal situation for growing succulents, they can certainly survive. Repot your plants if they begin to look as if they are struggling in a container without proper drainage.

If you water your indoor plants outdoors, be sure to keep them protected from direct sunlight, as the sudden change in sun exposure could shock them and cause the leaves to be scorched and scarred. On very slow-growing succulents, a sunburn can scar a plant for the remainder of its lifetime.

SUNLIGHT

In general, succulents do best in bright but indirect sunlight. A few hours of morning sun and indirect sunlight throughout the day is best. Different species can tolerate different amounts of light, but most tend to suffer in extended periods of direct sunlight. To avoid burning and scorching your plants, keep them in a place where they get shade but still receive adequate light. My healthiest plants are outside on windowsills, where they are protected from direct sunlight for most of the day by small overhangs. A few hours of direct sunlight is okay; just be sure your plants are sheltered from the harsh afternoon sun.

Experiment with your plants to see what works best where you live. The amount of sunlight succulents receive can affect the look of the plant. Succulents grown in full sun can become washed out and turn pinkish orange or even white, while the same plants grown in the shade will be more of a bluish green. If your plants are not getting enough light, they may become leggy and stretch toward the light. If your plants are stretching out or bending toward the light, you can slowly move them to a brighter spot or rotate their pots from time to time to keep them growing straight up. If your plant has grown too long, it may be time for you to propagate it (see the next chapter).

How to Overcome Common Problems with Succulents

Caring for your succulents' soil, water, and light exposure will help you avoid the majority of issues with succulents. Despite your best efforts, however, you might run into a problem once in a while, like you would with any other plant. Luckily, most trouble spots with succulents are easily identified and solved. Here are some potential trouble spots and how to fix them.

BUG INFESTATION

To avoid bug infestations and diseases in the first place, it's a good idea to remove any dead leaves from your plants, as they provide a perfect hiding place for pests and a breeding ground for fungi. Mealybugs, aphids, and spider mites are three common pests you may run into when growing succulents. If you have bugs in small numbers, they can be removed with a sharp pin or a strong stream of water. If you have a large infestation, you may need to use insecticidal sprays.

OVERWATERING

Succulents are designed to survive extended periods of drought, therefore they store water in their leaves. When they receive too much water, however, their leaves become very plump and swollen and may even rip open. If you have an overwatered succulent, cease watering it until the soil is completely dry.

ROT

Rot is a very common problem and goes hand in hand with overwatering. Fungi and bacteria tend to thrive in the fleshy tissue of succulents, so take special care to keep your plants in well-draining soil. If kept in moist, soggy soil, your plant will undoubtedly begin to rot.

SUNBURN

"Sunburns" happen when harsh sunlight causes a dark spot on a succulent's leaf. Succulents can become sunburnt very easily, especially when moved from shade to direct sunlight without being slowly acclimated. Sunburn can permanently scar a slow-growing succulent, so be very cautious of placing your plants in harsh sunlight.

Chapter 2

How to Propagate Succulents

What's propagation? Basically, creating new plants from seeds, leaves, cuttings, or other parts of existing plants. Many of the projects in this book will require cuttings, meaning you may need to cut an offshoot from its mother plant or cut a smaller plant from its root system. Taking succulent cuttings is a super easy way to multiply your plants with little time, effort, or money! Unlike flowers, which fade and wither away once cut, succulent cuttings will take root and thrive if given the proper care.

When to Propagate

Even if you keep succulents in bright windows that get plenty of light, they can sometimes still get "leggy." This happens when a plant isn't getting enough light and it starts to stretch out, causing the stem to grow long and the leaves to become widely spaced.

If you have a plant that is starting to become leggy like this one, have no fear. This is the perfect time to propagate!

Although your plant may still look gorgeous from the top, the lower leaves will begin to wither and fall off over time and you will be left with a rosette high above the soil on a long, bare stem. Before the leaves start to die, let's pull them off and propagate them to make more plants.

◀ Notice the long stem and widely spaced leaves.

◀ This plant is an ideal candidate for propagation because it still looks great from the top.

1. Collect Parts of the Plant

Remove the lower leaves first. Be really careful when you remove the leaves from the stem. I hold the leaf firmly and wiggle it from side to side until I feel a little snap. For most succulents, you can even just push the leaf in either direction with one finger and the leaf will come off. You want to be sure to get the entire leaf. If you rip the leaf, leaving the base still attached to the stem, it will not be able to grow roots or a new plant.

▶ Gently wiggle the leaf to remove it.

▶ This is what the leaves will look like if they are properly pulled from the stem remaining fully intact.

After you have successfully removed the lower leaves you will be left with a small rosette on a long, bare stem. This is where you will cut. I like to call the next step decapitation propagation. I'm not sure if that's the technical term, but it rhymes and we're going to cut its head off, so . . .

▲ I use a pair of craft scissors, but a sharp knife would work great as well.

▲ We now have a bunch of leaves, a stump, and a cute little plant with a short stem.

2. Let the Pieces Dry Out

Now, you wait. Before you can place the leaves and rosette in soil to begin growing new plants, you must let the ends dry out and callus over. This step is vital! If you don't let the ends dry out, they will absorb too much moisture, which will cause them to rot and die. The drying process could take anywhere from a few days to a week or so, depending on the type of plant and how thick the stem is.

▲ The freshly cut stem will be wet and fleshy.

▲ You will know you have waited long enough when the end of your stem has visibly dried out.

3. Place Leaves on Soil

Once the ends of the leaves have had time to callus over, you can place them on top of some well-draining cactus or succulent soil. (Some people dip the ends of the leaves and stem in a rooting hormone, but I've had great success without it.) Keep the leaves indoors in a window with lots of indirect sunlight. There is no need to water the ends of the leaves until you begin to see roots or baby plants growing from them.

After a few weeks, you will see little pink roots sprouting from the ends of the leaves. Then, teeny tiny baby plants will begin to grow. It will look like a miniature succulent sprouting from the end of the leaf.

Once you see roots or baby plants, leave them lying on top of the soil and you may begin watering. Give them a good soak about once a week or whenever the soil is totally dry. Just as with a fully developed succulent, too much water is not good. If you want to be certain not to overwater, mist the roots growing from your leaves with a spray bottle once a day instead of completely saturating the soil.

Finally, Repot the New Plants

Let the baby plants grow until you notice the "mother leaf" starting to wither. At that point, you can carefully remove the leaf in the same fashion you removed it from the original stem, and then place the baby plant in its own pot. Removing the original leaf can be tricky, as you don't want to accidentally remove the roots with the leaf. If you give it a gentle wiggle and it doesn't come off, you may want to play it safe and let the leaf fall off on its own.

Keep in mind, not every leaf will grow a new plant. I've found that some leaves just wither away, some will take root while never growing a new plant, and some might even grow a plant but never root. Although there will typically be a small amount of losses, most leaves will grow roots followed by a new plant.

▲ A plant with roots.

▲ This leaf grew a baby plant first and no roots.

▲ I ran out of individual little pots with this batch, so I just removed the leaves as they withered and left the plants to grow together like a little succulent forest.

4. Don't Forget about the Original Stump!

Okay, back to that stump. Don't worry, no part of this plant is going to go to waste!

Simply put this pot aside and eventually it will begin to sprout new plants. Babies may potentially grow from each place we removed a leaf!

New growth. ▶

5. Plant the Cutting

Now back to our cutting, the reason we did all of this! Once the stem has dried out and callused over, simply place the plant back in a pot with well-draining cactus or succulent soil and it will grow roots again and continue to flourish!

Part 2

PROJECTS

Chapter 3

For the Home

Succulents can add interest and personality when used as decor throughout your home. There are so many ways to style them—you can plant a succulent in almost any container. In this chapter, we will create twelve unique succulent projects that can be used in and around your home from materials you may already have on hand.

It's really important to keep in mind that succulents do best in bright but not harsh direct light. Find a place in your home where your plants will receive plenty of light throughout the day. If your plants do not receive adequate light, they could become leggy as they stretch toward the sun.

SUCCULENTS IN TEACUPS

Planting succulents in your old teacups is a fun and easy way to freshen up a classic piece of kitchenware. Most people have at least a couple of teacups in the cupboard and if not, you can find them relatively cheap at most thrift stores. The options are almost endless: Add a few teacup succulents to your kitchen window to create an indoor teacup garden. Need a last-minute gift idea? Grab a teacup, plant a small succulent in it, and voila! If you are new to gardening or crafting with succulents, this is a great project to start with.

WHAT YOU NEED

- ○ Teacup
- ○ Pebbles
- ○ Soil
- ○ Succulents
- ○ Moss (Optional)

WHAT TO DO

1 Pour a layer of pebbles into your teacup. About an inch or so should be plenty.

2 Fill your teacup about ¾ full with well-draining cactus/succulent soil.

3 Use your fingers to push the soil up against the sides of the teacup, creating a hole in the middle of the soil for the plant's roots to fit into.

4 Carefully hold your plant sideways by its base and slide it out of its current container. Remove any excess soil from the roots. Try your best not to handle the leaves of the plant too much as they may be easily scarred.

5 Plant your succulent by setting the roots of the plant into the hole you created, and carefully fill the rest of the teacup with soil. Press the soil down around the stem to secure the plant into position.

6   If desired, plant multiple succulents to create a small arrangement within that teacup.

CARE INSTRUCTIONS

Teacups do not have proper drainage holes, so be careful not to over-water your succulents. Stick a finger down into the soil to be sure the soil is completely dry before each watering.

TIP!
Add pebbles or moss to the top of your soil to give your arrangement a finished look.

SUCCULENTS IN PAINTED MASON JARS

Mason jars are being used more than ever in crafting and decor because they are so easy to customize. If you don't have any jars on hand, it's easy to find them at grocery or home stores nowadays. Whether you are repurposing an old jar or using a brand-new one, Mason jars lend a vintage, upcycled feel to your home.

WHAT YOU NEED

- ○ Mason Jar
- ○ Paint
- ○ Foam Paintbrush
- ○ Sandpaper or Nail File
- ○ Pebbles
- ○ Soil
- ○ Succulents

WHAT TO DO

1 Hold your Mason jar upside down—place your hand inside the jar if you can. With your other hand, paint the jar in your desired color using vertical strokes. You may need to apply a couple of coats depending on how thick your paint is. Allow your paint to dry completely between coats.

2 If you want your jars to have a distressed look to them, use your sandpaper or nail file to gently remove some of the paint where the jar would most likely get worn over time.

3 Prepare your jar for planting. Start by adding an inch or two of pebbles followed by your soil. Make sure to leave enough room for the roots of your plant to fit into the jar.

4 Plant your succulents. Create a little hole in the soil for your plant to fit into. Place your plant in the jar and cover the roots with soil.

CARE INSTRUCTIONS

Since Mason jars do not have proper drainage, take care not to overwater the succulents in them. Stick a finger down into the soil to be sure the soil is completely dry before each watering.

TIP!

Try wrapping your jars with jute twine for a natural, earthy feel or get fancy by using burlap and lace! Screw on the jar's open lid for an extra touch if desired.

SUCCULENTS IN WINE CORKS

Using wine corks as decor is an inexpensive (possibly even free) way to add some sophistication to your home or event. You can upcycle your used wine corks or purchase unused corks at a craft store. Cork planters create a cute and classy way to display tiny plants you've propagated yourself. These make great favors for your next wine-tasting party or book club!

WHAT YOU NEED

- ○ Wine Corks
- ○ Drill
- ○ ¼" Drill Bit
- ○ Soil
- ○ Pencil or similar pointy tool
- ○ Baby Succulents

CARE INSTRUCTIONS

Keep your cork planters in bright indirect sunlight and water every couple of days. Only a small amount of soil will fit in your cork, so it will dry out quickly.

WHAT TO DO

1 Drill a hole as deep into your cork as possible without drilling all the way through.

2 Fill the hole with succulent soil.

3 Choose a small succulent to plant in your cork.

4 Use a pencil or other long pointy tool to create a hole in your soil for the stem and roots of your plant to fit into.

5 Plant your succulent!

TIP!

Get creative and add interest to your wine cork planters by gluing moss to the tops, or create cute hanging planters by adding magnetic strips to the backs. You might even use them as little centerpieces by tying multiple cork planters together with twine!

SUCCULENT TERRARIUM

Terrariums come in all shapes and sizes and make a stunning design element in your home or office. Really, any open glass container can be used as a succulent terrarium. Whether you choose a bowl, geometric shape, or glass bubble, your succulent terrarium will make a huge impact. You can find interesting terrariums at World Market, Urban Outfitters, or stores online. In this project, I added a cactus, another type of succulent.

○ Glass Container

○ Rocks or Pebbles

○ Activated Charcoal

○ Sphagnum Moss

○ Soil

○ Succulents

○ Sand (Optional)

○ Decorative Accessories

○ Spoon, Tweezers, Straw (Optional)

WHAT TO DO

1 Start by lining the bottom of the terrarium with rocks or pebbles and a thin layer of activated charcoal. Since succulents prefer containers with good drainage, the pebbles will create a space for water to drain out of the soil. This will keep the plants' roots from sitting in excess water and will prevent rot. The activated charcoal acts as a filter for the soil and water. It can freshen the air in the terrarium, which is especially useful if your container has a small opening, and it can also draw bacteria from your soil and water.

2 Add a layer of sphagnum moss between your pebbles and soil to prevent the soil from running down into the rocks over time. Sphagnum moss will also assist in creating an alternative drainage system, providing a place for water to escape from the soil.

3 Mix a few tablespoons of activated charcoal with your well-draining soil and add the soil mixture to the terrarium.

4 Decide which plants you would like to use for your terrarium. If you are using cuttings, make sure to take them a few days prior to making your terrarium. To avoid rot, you will want to give the ends time to dry out and callus over before planting them in soil.

CARE INSTRUCTIONS

Place your terrarium in indirect sunlight. Glass magnifies light and heat, so be careful not to place your terrarium where it will receive a lot of direct sunlight. Stick a finger down into the soil to be sure the soil is completely dry before each watering.

5 Begin adding plants and decorations to your terrarium. You may want to use sand on top of the soil for aesthetic value. Depending on the size of the opening of your terrarium, you may find it easier to add the sand before the plants. If you plant your succulents first, use a spoon to pour the sand around the plants.

6 Next, add any decorative moss, pebbles, and twigs you want. If the opening on your terrarium is quite small, you can use tweezers to add moss to the areas where your fingers can't reach. Use a straw to gently blow sand and soil off of the plants and glass.

TIP!

A terrarium is usually a sealable glass container used to create a small-scale ecosystem for plants. When creating a succulent terrarium, though, you will want to find a container that is open to the atmosphere. Succulents should be planted in open containers since they prefer low humidity and dry soil, as opposed to the moist environment a closed terrarium provides.

SUCCULENTS IN DECORATED TERRA COTTA POTS

Terra cotta pots are readily available and are an inexpensive option for holding succulents. They come in many different sizes—from itty bitty for your baby plants to large enough to hold a gorgeous arrangement of multiple succulents. I love how they become aged over time, creating a rustic and unique look for each individual pot. There are countless ways to decorate terra cotta pots, but using paint, jute twine, and lace are three of my favorites!

WHAT YOU NEED

- ○ Terra Cotta Pots
- ○ Outdoor Paint
- ○ Paintbrush
- ○ Scissors
- ○ Lace
- ○ Jute Twine
- ○ Hot Glue
- ○ Soil
- ○ Succulents

WHAT TO DO

1 **TO PAINT YOUR TERRA COTTA POTS:** There are different ways to go about painting pots:

- I find it easiest to use spray paint when I want to paint an entire pot. You may also tape off designs when using spray paint as well.
- You can also paint them with a paintbrush.
- You might also like to try dipping your pots in paint. Simply open a gallon of paint and dip your pots. You'll need to use a paintbrush to remove any excess paint and let the paint drip off into the paint container. Once all of the excess paint has dripped off, set your pots aside to dry. The paint is pretty thick when you use the dipping technique, so you may want to hang your pots to dry if possible.

2 **TO ADD LACE:** Once the paint is completely dry, add lace to the rim. Cut a strip of lace to fit around the upper rim of your pot and use hot glue to hold it in place.

3 **TO ADD JUTE TWINE:** Hot-glue the twine to your pot as you wrap it around to keep the jute in place. You can wrap your entire pot or just part of it.

4 Once you've decorated the pots to your liking, fill them with well-draining soil and plant your succulents in them. You can plant one plant in each pot or create arrangements with multiple succulents.

CARE INSTRUCTIONS

Place your decorated pots in a place where they will receive bright, indirect sunlight throughout the day. Water when the soil is completely dry.

SUCCULENT ADDRESS PLAQUE

First impressions are lasting, so what better way to welcome guests into your home than with a beautiful succulent address plaque? Your visitors will know they're in the right place when they see your house number, and they will immediately be greeted by a stunning arrangement of fresh, eye-catching succulents. They won't believe you when they find out you "did it yourself"!

WHAT YOU NEED

- 14" x 11" Pine Wood Plaque
- Two pieces of 0.25" x 3" x 9.5" Pine Craft Wood
- Two pieces of 0.25" x 3.25" x 3" Pine Craft Wood
- Staple Gun and ½" (12mm) Heavy-Duty Staples
- Drill (Optional)
- Tape Measure
- Pencil
- Hammer

- Finishing Nails
- Wood Glue
- Cloth or Towel
- Outdoor Spray Paint or Stain
- Frame Hangers
- Address Numbers
- Plastic Wrap
- Soil
- Succulents

1 You can make the planting box whatever dimensions you want, depending on how much room you want the succulent box to take up on the plaque. For these instructions, I'll show you how to make what's shown in the photo.

2 Staple your 3.25" × 3" wood pieces to the ends of your 3" × 9.5" rectangular wood pieces to create the sides of your succulent box. (Since you're using craft wood, the staples from a staple gun will go right through it.) The plaque itself will be the back side of the box.

3   If you want your succulent box to have drainage holes, drill them now. (If, for some reason, you don't want water draining under your plaque, don't drill the holes.)

4   Flip your 14" × 11" wood plaque over so that the back is facing up. We are going to trace the outline of the succulent box on the back of the plaque so we can hammer in the nails where the box will go.

5   Position your succulent box and measure it to be sure it is aligned with the edges of the plaque. Holding the box in place, trace around the outside, and then around the inside, of the box with a pencil and then remove the box. Measure again to be sure the lines are aligned with the edges of the plaque.

6 Hammer your finishing nails through the plaque between the inner and the outer lines that you traced. Two nails on the sides, and three across the bottom will suffice.

7 Flip your plaque over so that the front is facing up. You should now have the pointed ends of your finishing nails sticking through in the shape of your succulents box.

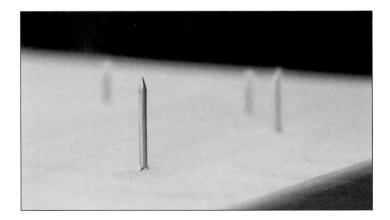

8   Apply wood glue to the back edges of your box and press the edges of the box onto the nails.

9   Cover the front of your box with a cloth or towel and lightly hammer the box into the nails until the box sits flush with the plaque.

10 If you'd like, you can now spray-paint your address plaque and planting box with outdoor paint. You can also stain your plaque or paint it with a brush, but I found spray-painting it to be the easiest.

11 Once your paint dries, attach your frame hangers to the back of the plaque. Estimate how much your plaque will weigh with the soil and plants in it and be sure to purchase a hanger that can handle that weight. (Follow the directions that came with your hangers for this.)

12 Now attach your house numbers to the plaque. House numbers come in many different fonts, sizes, colors, and materials. I liked these "floating" numbers with a modern feel, but you can choose anything that matches your style.

13 Line your succulent box with plastic wrap to protect the wood. You can glue it into place if it's slipping around too much. If you drilled drainage holes, pop holes in the plastic with a pencil or another pointy tool.

14 Fill your succulent box with well-draining succulent soil and plant your succulents. Be sure not to cover your numbers with tall plants.

CARE INSTRUCTIONS

Place your address plaque in bright, indirect sunlight and water when the soil is dry. If your plants grow vertically, by sure to keep them trimmed so they don't block your house numbers.

LETTER SUCCULENT GARDEN

Get personal by creating a custom, letter-shaped succulent garden. Kept horizontally, it will make a lovely centerpiece, or hang it vertically for stunning wall art. First or last name initials are popular choices, or maybe you'd like to create multiple succulent letter gardens to spell out a word, such as "LOVE." We will be using old pallet wood for this project. Many hardware stores will sell you their old pallets for a few dollars. Old fence wood can also be used.

WHAT YOU NEED

- ○ Pallet Wood
- ○ Thin Plywood
- ○ Tape Measure
- ○ Saw
- ○ Staple Gun and Staples
- ○ Drill
- ○ ¼" Drill Bit
- ○ Sandpaper
- ○ Mesh Wire (Optional)
- ○ Sphagnum Moss
- ○ Soil
- ○ Succulents

WHAT TO DO

1 Choose a letter that you would like to turn into a succulent planter. It can be any letter, but remember that curvy letters will take more skill to create out of wood then straight-sided letters. For frame of reference, my letter here is about 1 foot wide and just over a foot long.

2 If your pallet isn't already dismantled, you will need to do that at this time. Taking a pallet apart by removing the nails holding it together is no easy task, so you may want to do what I did and just saw the wood directly off the pallet. My pallet had been out in the weather for quite some time and was really brittle. Rather then destroy the wood by prying it apart with a hammer or crowbar, I decided it would be easier to saw off the wood pieces I needed to create the letter while the pallet was still intact.

3 Measure, cut, and staple together the wood pieces that you removed from your pallet to create your letter. These pieces will be the sides of your planter. I stapled my pieces together on the back and sides of the letter so that no staples would be visible from the front.

4   Trace your letter onto the thin plywood. This will serve as the backing for your letter.

5   Cut out your letter with a saw and drill some holes in it to create some drainage.

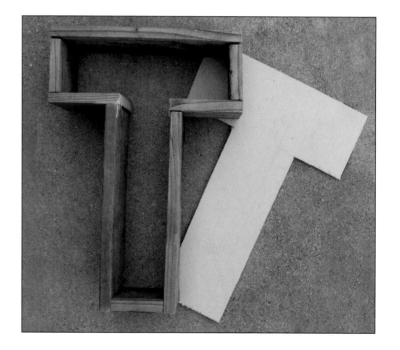

6 Use your sandpaper to smooth out any really rough edges on the letter backing.

7 Flip your pallet wood letter over so that the front side is down, and staple on your plywood backing.

8 If you plan to hang your letter vertically, now is the time to add your hanging hardware. Follow the instructions included with your specific hardware. Be sure to estimate how much the letter will weigh with the soil in it so you can purchase a hanger that can handle its weight.

9 Line the bottom with sphagnum moss to create a barrier between the soil and wood.

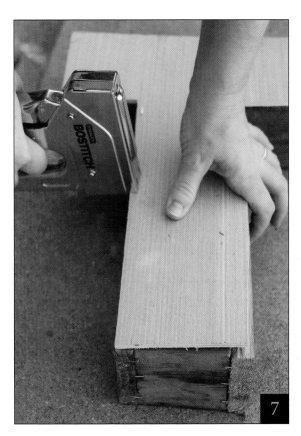

10 Depending on the size of your letter, whether you will be setting it up horizontally or vertically, and whether you will be using entire plants or cuttings, you may want to staple some wire mesh to the front of your letter. Add the wire before you put soil in, since the soil and cuttings can fit through the wire.

11 Fill the letter with soil.

12 Plant your succulents. Choose a color scheme or a few types of plants, but use different sizes to create visual interest.

13 If your letter is going to be a vertical garden, you will need to let your plants take root for a few weeks before standing it up or hanging it. After a few weeks, gently pull on your plants to see if they come out of the soil easily. If they are not secure in the soil, you may need to wait a few weeks longer.

CARE INSTRUCTIONS

Place your letter garden where it will receive bright but indirect sunlight. If it is being kept vertical, you will need to lay it horizontal when you water. Water when the soil is totally dry and let the water completely drain out before you hang or stand it back up.

SUCCULENT KOKEDAMA

Kokedama first originated in Japan, where these moss ball string gardens are very popular. Kokedama is a unique and easy way to grow plants in and around your home and garden. Like other vertical gardens, kokedama are visually interesting while saving space at the same time. They make earthy accent pieces to an outdoor gathering—they're sure to get guests talking!

WHAT YOU NEED

- ○ Sheet Moss
- ○ Scissors
- ○ Soil
- ○ Bowl of Water
- ○ Succulent
- ○ String or Twine

WHAT TO DO

1   Use your scissors to create a circle from your sheet moss. (You can find sheet moss at most garden centers.)

2   Wet your soil, creating a claylike consistency. Use your hands to create a ball with the soil. Squeeze excess water out as you form the ball.

3   Place the ball of soil on your sheet moss. Hold the ball gently in your hands while using your thumbs to create a hole in the top of the ball where you are going to plant your succulent.

4 Plant your succulent in the top of the ball of soil.

5 Wrap your sheet moss around the ball.

6 Tuck the moss under the plant's lowest leaves.

7 If your circle is too big and you have too much moss, simply cut away the surplus until the moss fits neatly under the leaves at the top.

8 Take your string and begin wrapping the ball in any direction. Your goal is simply to keep the moss together with the soil ball, but you can make it look any way you like aesthetically! Get creative with the way you wrap your moss ball. You can use any color string, rope, twine, yarn, or even leather. Make sure to leave at least 12 inches of string at the beginning and enough string at the end that you can tie the two ends together for hanging once your ball is completely wrapped.

9 Cut the string with your scissors and tie the ends together. Now find a place to hang your kokedama.

CARE INSTRUCTIONS

Hang your kokedama in bright indirect sunlight and soak the ball in water when the soil is dry.

SUCCULENT COLANDER

Whether you are preparing a meal, helping kids with homework, or simply enjoying a cup of coffee with friends, the kitchen often ends up being the hub of a household. Your succulents will feel right at home in your kitchen when planted in a brightly colored colander.

WHAT YOU NEED

- ○ Colander
- ○ Plastic Wrap
- ○ Hot Glue
- ○ Pencil or similar pointy tool
- ○ Pebbles (Optional)
- ○ Soil
- ○ Succulents
- ○ Decorative Sand

WHAT TO DO

1 Start by lining your colander with some plastic. Secure it in place with hot glue. You don't want your soil escaping through all the holes!

2 Use a sharpened pencil to poke a couple of holes in your plastic where there are already holes in the colander. This will create a way for water to drain. (If you don't want drainage holes for some reason—such as not wanting water to drip out of the bottom onto your kitchen counter—line the bottom of your colander with pebbles and skip this step.)

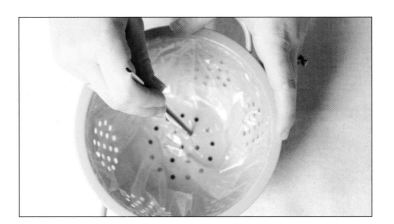

3   Fill your colander about ¾ full of soil.

4   Begin adding your succulents. As you plant them, add more soil around each plant until the colander is full of plants and soil.

5   Cover your soil with decorative sand if you prefer the look.

CARE INSTRUCTIONS

Place your succulent colander in bright, indirect sunlight and water when the soil is completely dry.

TINY TERRA COTTA MAGNETS

Looking for an adorable way to display your tiniest succulents? Look no further. Tiny terra cotta pots are the cutest way to show off your babies. Itty-bitty pots are charming in their own right, but when paired with darling little succulents, the cuteness factor is off the charts! Add magnets to the back of your pots to hang them on your fridge or around the house on other metal surfaces. These make an adorable gift for a teacher, neighbor, or friend.

WHAT YOU NEED

- ○ ½" Magnets
- ○ Glue Gun and Glue
- ○ Tiny Terra Cotta Pots, less than 1" tall
- ○ Soil
- ○ Baby Succulents

WHAT TO DO

1. Use your glue gun to add some glue to one of the magnets.

2. Press the magnet onto one of the mini terra cotta pots.

3. Add soil to the pot and plant a baby succulent in it. Repeat steps 1 through 3 for the remaining pots and plants.

CARE INSTRUCTIONS

Since your tiny pots don't hold much soil, they need to be watered regularly. Water every few days or when you notice the soil is totally dry. Keep your little pots where they get bright, indirect sunlight if possible. If your pot magnets are on the fridge and your plants start to stretch toward the sun, simply remove the leggy plant and replace it with a new one. These containers are more of a novelty than a permanent home for growing succulents.

TIP!

Get crafty with your kids by letting them paint some mini pots. They will love adding a touch of personalization and then seeing their little works of art hanging on the fridge!

BIRCH LOG PLANTER

Planting succulents in a birch log is a perfect way to add a natural, rustic element to your home. Birchwood is easy to find at most home stores or garden centers. This planter also makes a unique centerpiece for a wedding or event.

WHAT YOU NEED

○ 6"–8" Tall Birch Log
○ Drill with Blade Bit
○ Plastic Wrap
○ Pebbles
○ Soil
○ Succulents
○ Hot or Floral Glue
○ Moss

CARE INSTRUCTIONS

Place your log planter in an area of your home that receives bright but indirect sunlight and a few hours of direct sunlight throughout the day. Water when the soil is completely dry.

WHAT TO DO

1 Use your drill with a blade bit to drill a hole into your log. You want the hole to be big enough for the roots of your plants to fit with some extra soil.

2 Line the hole in your log with plastic to protect the wood from water damage. You may want to glue the plastic into place if it's slipping around too much.

3 Add a layer of pebbles (for drainage), soil, and your plants.

4 Attach moss to the log with your glue to add the finishing touch.

TIP!
Try using this same technique on a variety of logs in and around your home. Drill holes in larger logs to use as planters in your garden.

LIVING WREATH

Add beauty to your home with a breathtaking succulent wreath. It's also very versatile—you can hang it vertically on your front door, or lay it flat as a centerpiece with a tall candle in the center. Easily customizable, this wreath is sure to be a delight for years to come. It makes a lovely housewarming gift!

WHAT YOU NEED

○ Sphagnum Moss
○ Large Bowl of Water
○ Wreath Frame 13"–15"
○ Jute Twine
○ Scissors
○ Pencil or similar pointy tool
○ Succulent Cuttings
○ Floral Pins
○ Wreath Hanger

WHAT TO DO

1 Soak your sphagnum moss in a large bowl of water.

2 Begin adding your moss to your wreath frame, squeezing out any excess water as you go.

3 As you work your way around the wreath frame, press the moss together as if you are creating a loaf.

4 Once the entire wreath frame is covered with moss, tie the end of the jute twine to the back of the frame and wrap the moss with the twine. This will keep the moss attached to your frame. Once you have gone around the entire frame once or twice, tie off and cut your jute twine.

5 Use your pencil or other pointy tool to create holes in the moss for your succulent cuttings to fit into. Use your floral pins to fasten your cuttings into place if necessary.

6 Work your way around the wreath, arranging plants to suit your liking. I chose to group certain types of plants together. Pick one or two larger plants to serve as visual focal points.

CARE INSTRUCTIONS

Place your wreath where it will get enough sunlight to keep the plants from stretching out and becoming leggy, but not *too* much direct sunlight, as this can burn your succulent cuttings. Water your wreath by submerging it in water when the sphagnum moss becomes dry. This will probably be about once a week, depending on the weather where you live.

7 Allow plants to dry and root for a few weeks before hanging the wreath vertically with the wreath hanger.

Chapter 4

In the Garden

Succulents are a modern and water-wise way to beautify your garden. They complement almost any landscaping, and can also be used to enhance your typical garden decor. The wonderful thing about planting your succulents in containers, rather than in the ground, is that you can easily move them around your garden as the seasons change, providing them with the best possible living conditions. If an arrangement is receiving too much or not enough light, simply move it to a more suitable position. In this chapter, we will be creating nine unique projects that can be tailored to match your home's garden style—whether you have 10 acres of land or an urban windowsill.

SUCCULENT BIRDCAGE

Birdcages are a classic garden accessory. You may have seen them filled with candles or overflowing with flowers, but nothing is quite as showstopping as a birdcage spilling over with gorgeous, cascading succulents. Look for inexpensive vintage birdcages at local antique shops or garage sales.

WHAT YOU NEED

- ○ Birdcage
- ○ Moss
- ○ Pebbles
- ○ Soil
- ○ Succulents

WHAT TO DO

1 Line the perimeter of your birdcage with moss to create a barrier to keep your soil inside.

2 Add a layer of pebbles and well-draining soil.

3 Plant succulents in your birdcage. Use cascading succulents around the perimeter of the birdcage for dramatic effect.

CARE INSTRUCTIONS

Place your birdcage in an area of your garden that receives bright but indirect sunlight and a few hours of direct sunlight throughout the day. Water when the soil is completely dry.

TIP!
Customize your birdcage by spray-painting it one of your favorite colors before you add your succulents.

VERTICAL FRAMED SUCCULENT GARDEN

It's no wonder vertical succulent gardens are rising in popularity—they are easy to customize, don't take up valuable ground space, and can be decorated to your liking. Whether you are an urban gardener with limited space or simply want to create some living art, vertical succulent gardens are a sophisticated way to add a one-of-a-kind accent to your garden.

WHAT YOU NEED

- 8" x 10" Wood Picture Frame
- Mesh Wire
- Wire Cutters
- Two Pieces of ¼" x 1.5" x 8" Craft Wood
- Two Pieces of ¼" x 1.5" x 10" Craft Wood
- Staple Gun and Staples
- Moss
- Saw
- Thin Plywood
- Frame Hooks (Optional)
- Soil
- Pencil or similar pointy tool
- Succulent Cuttings

WHAT TO DO

1 Since the frame itself is shallow, you'll need to use cuttings instead of full plants. Refer to Chapter 2 for how to propagate succulents. This should be done a few days prior to planting to ensure that your stems have had time to callus over. Once your succulents have callused, you are ready to begin this project.

2 Place your frame face down on your workspace. Cut your mesh wire to fit the back opening of your frame and lay it in the opening. When you staple the sides of the box to the frame, the wire gets trapped there and will hold.

3 Now we'll make extra support for the inside of the frame, to hold the soil. Take your ¼" pieces of craft wood and staple them to the inside lips of your frame, trapping the wire mesh between the back of the frame and the wood pieces.

4   This is what the back of the completed frame looks like.

5   Cut your plywood to the dimensions of the opening and staple to the wood sides, creating a bottom for your soil box.

6   At this point, you may want to add a wire, frame hooks, or another hanging mechanism to the back of your frame, if you plan to hang it once the cuttings have rooted.

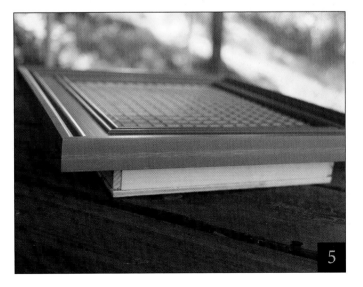

7 Turn your frame over so it's right-side up and add soil through the mesh wire. Use your hand to push the soil through the mesh wire. Shake the frame to settle the soil, making room for more.

8 Use a pencil (or similar pointy tool) to create a hole in the soil for the stem of your plant.

9   Begin planting your succulent cuttings.

10   You are creating a living work of art, so be creative with your design. Make it interesting by grouping similar plants together, add one or two larger plants to catch the viewer's eye, or create waves of similar plants.

11 Use your moss to fill in any empty space and to cover any mesh wire that may be showing.

12 Keep your frame horizontal for about six weeks, or until roots have established. You can check this by looking for new growth or tugging lightly on your plants. If the plants remove easily from the soil, they need more time to take root.

13 Once your plants have taken root, choose where you will hang your masterpiece.

CARE INSTRUCTIONS

Your frame will do best with bright, filtered, or indirect sunlight throughout the day. If you hang the frame indoors, place it near a south-facing window. You will need to lay the frame horizontally when you water. Water it about every two weeks (monthly when it's colder) or when the soil is totally dry. Let the soil fully drain before replacing the frame on the wall. Remove dried leaves periodically to keep your frame planter looking its best!

TIP!

If you are hanging your vertical garden on a wall, it's a good idea to add a frame hook to each side of your frame, giving you the option to rotate it every couple of weeks. Over time, succulents tend to grow toward the sun. To keep your plants from stretching in a certain direction, rotate the frame often.

SUCCULENT BIRD NEST

Tucking a succulent-filled bird nest into some branches in your garden is a charming way to display your plants. Your nest will be an organic and natural-feeling addition to your outdoor space. You can find a variety of nests at local craft stores. This is a great piece to feature in springtime.

WHAT YOU NEED

- ⭘ Nest, approximately 10" in diameter
- ⭘ Moss
- ⭘ Soil
- ⭘ Succulents
- ⭘ Plastic Bird or Eggs

WHAT TO DO

1 Line your nest with moss to keep your soil from falling through the twigs over time.

2 Fill your nest with well-draining soil.

3   Plants succulents in your nest.

4   Add decorative accessories, such as a plastic bird or eggs.

CARE INSTRUCTIONS

Place your bird nest in an area of your garden that receives bright but indirect sunlight and a few hours of direct sunlight throughout the day. Water when the soil is completely dry.

VERTICAL PALLET SHELF GARDEN

Any kind of vertical garden is a great space saver and can add interest to your outdoor space without taking up too much precious ground space. This pallet garden is easy to construct— you can even find small pallets like this one at craft stores. Feel free to customize this gem by painting or staining it. Whether you upcycle an old pallet or purchase a new one, it's sure to be one of your favorite garden accessories.

WHAT YOU NEED

- ○ Pallet
- ○ Landscape Fabric
- ○ Scissors
- ○ Staple Gun and Staples
- ○ Plywood (if necessary)
- ○ Soil
- ○ Succulents

WHAT TO DO

1 If your pallet is not the size you want it to be, first cut it down to the size you want.

2 You are going to start off by creating "shelves" out of your landscape fabric. Cut strips that are a little bit longer and wider than the inside area of each level so that you can staple them to the insides of the pallet slats.

3 Staple your landscape fabric to the inside of the pallet. If you want your pallet garden to be aesthetically pleasing from all angles, be sure not to staple the fabric to the outside of the pallet. My pallet was purchased at a craft store and had an open back. This made stapling the landscape fabric into place a breeze. If your pallet does not have an open back, you may need to remove a couple of slats to get a good angle with your staple gun.

4. If your pallet has an open back, you will need to enclose it with wood slats. (If you removed slats to add the fabric, simply staple them back into place.) You can create new slats by cutting any comparable wood (I used a thin plywood) to match the size of your existing slats and then staple them into place.

5. Fill each level with a well-draining succulent soil.

6. Choose and arrange your succulents. Since this pallet garden uses a shelving system, you can plant your succulents in the shelves vertically and they are ready to go from day one (no waiting for roots to take hold before hanging!). Look for cascading succulents or plants that will grow outward from the pallet.

CARE INSTRUCTIONS

Place your pallet in an area of your garden that receives bright but indirect sunlight and a few hours of direct sunlight throughout the day. Water when the soil is completely dry.

TIP!

Take advantage of having an open shelf system in your pallet garden! If you prefer to have your pallet visible from the front and back, you can plant succulents on the reverse side as well.

BIRDBATH

Birdbaths are a quintessential piece of garden decor that helps you create an enchanting space. Planting succulents in your birdbath will take a classic garden design element and make it new and interesting.

WHAT YOU NEED

- Birdbath
- Pebbles
- Soil
- Succulents

WHAT TO DO

1 Line the bottom of your birdbath with pebbles to assist in drainage.

2 Fill your birdbath with soil.

3　Arrange your succulents. Pick two or three bigger succulents as attention-grabbing centerpieces and surround with smaller filler plants. Use some cascading succulents over the edges of the birdbath.

CARE INSTRUCTIONS

Place your birdbath in an area of your garden that receives bright but indirect sunlight and a few hours of direct sunlight throughout the day. Water when the soil is completely dry.

CINDERBLOCK GARDEN

Cinderblock gardens are perfect for the urban gardener with limited space, or the design-conscious gardener with a modern flair. The softness of the plants takes the edge off what might otherwise be a stark part of your landscape. The concrete blocks make perfect containers for succulents, and the wire screen bottoms you'll add provide excellent drainage.

WHAT YOU NEED

- ○ Cinderblocks
- ○ Wire Cutters
- ○ Wire Screen
- ○ Soil
- ○ Succulents

WHAT TO DO

1   Decide on a formation for your cinderblock garden. Get creative!

2   Use your wire cutters to cut your wire screen to the dimensions of your cinderblocks.

3   Place your wire screen under the highest cinderblock on each level of your garden. This will save a lot of soil.

4   Fill only the cinderblocks that will hold plants with soil and plant
    your succulents in them. Choose plants of different sizes, colors,
    and textures to create visual interest. Add cascading succulents to
    the highest blocks.

CARE INSTRUCTIONS

Place your cinderblock garden in an area that receives bright but indirect sunlight and a few hours of direct sunlight throughout the day. Water when the soil is completely dry.

BIRDHOUSE

Birdhouses are a fun and functional way to add charm to your garden while providing shelter for a feathered friend. The woodsy moss and gorgeous succulents will have the birds in your garden fighting over this prized real estate!

WHAT YOU NEED

- Wood Birdhouse
- Six pieces of ¼"-thick Craft Wood
- Tape Measure
- Saw
- Staple Gun and Staples
- Mesh Hardware Cloth
- Wire Cutters

- Succulent Soil
- Sphagnum Moss
- Pencil or similar pointy tool
- Succulent Cuttings
- Floral Pins
- Hot Glue
- Decorative Moss

WHAT TO DO

1. Measure and cut your ¼"-thick craft wood to the lengths of the sides of your birdhouse's roof. You will need two smaller pieces for the bases of the roof and four longer pieces for the sides.

2. Staple your craft wood pieces to the roof of your birdhouse, creating rooftop boxes to hold your succulents. Try to staple from angles where the staples will not be visible from the front.

3. Now, measure the pitch of your roof and cut a piece of mesh wire hardware cloth that will fit over the top of your new succulent box.

4 Staple your mesh wire to your succulent box, creating a new roof.

5 Fill the slopes of your roof with soil. If you would rather not use soil, you can fill the entire succulent box with sphagnum moss.

6   Fill empty space at the peak of your roof with sphagnum moss.

7   Use a pencil or similar pointy tool to create a hole in the soil or moss where you want to insert your succulent cutting.

8 Begin planting your succulents. Use floral pins to hold your plants in place if necessary.

9 Plant a larger succulent in the sphagnum moss at the peak of your birdhouse facing forward.

10 Hot-glue moss to the edges of your roof to hide any mesh wire that may still be showing.

CARE INSTRUCTIONS

Place your succulent-topped birdhouse where it will receive plenty of bright, indirect sunlight. Water when the soil is dry.

SUCCULENT CHAIR

A chair planter is a great way to add character to your garden. This DIY came about because we found these cute metal chairs, but no pots or baskets would fit into the seat opening. So, of course, when you can't buy, you've gotta DIY! Metal chair pot-holders like this one are available at some garden centers and online.

WHAT YOU NEED

- Metal Chair
- Coconut Fiber Planter Liner
- Screwdriver
- Jute Twine
- Transparent Tape
- Scissors
- Soil
- Succulents

WHAT TO DO

1 Start by fitting your coconut fiber planter liner into the seat hole of your chair. If your liner is too big, simply fold it so that it overlaps and fits into the opening.

2 Take your liner out and use a screwdriver to create holes along the upper edge. Be sure not to place your holes too close to the edge.

3   Tie one end of your jute twine to the rim of the chair and wrap the other end with tape to keep it from fraying. You will be using the twine to "sew" your liner to the chair, so make sure you give yourself plenty of length to work with.

4   Begin sewing your liner to the rim of your chair. You may need to use your screwdriver to reopen the holes along the way if the twine doesn't easily fit into the holes.

5 Once you have made it all the way around the circle, tie your twine and cut off any remaining length.

6 Lightly fill your awesome new chair planter with soil. Don't pack it in tightly, as you don't want to stretch out the liner.

7 Plant your succulents! Start by adding your tallest plants in the back and work your way forward. Choose two or three plants to be your attention-grabbers, or focal points. They can be brightly colored or slightly bigger than the other plants to set them apart. Fill in any empty space with smaller plants so that you don't have a lot of soil showing.

CARE INSTRUCTIONS

Place your succulent-filled chair where it will receive plenty of bright, indirect sunlight. Water when the soil is dry.

TIP!

Over time, the coconut fiber liner may thin because of the weight of the soil and plants. It's a good idea to reinforce your liner. You can do this by looping your twine all the way under the liner, creating a support system. If you don't like the look of the twine against the coconut fiber, try using clear fishing wire.

POTTED PALLET GARDEN

Everyone loves the look of an upcycled pallet, but sometimes heavy pallet gardens can be hard to relocate. If you're like me and prefer to move your plants around your garden throughout the year, this potted pallet garden is a great option. Not only is it lighter in weight than a typical pallet garden, but your pots can be rotated, giving your plants even sun exposure to keep them from stretching toward the sun.

WHAT YOU NEED

- ○ Galvanized Steel Hanger Tape
- ○ Terra Cotta Pots
- ○ Tin Snips
- ○ Measuring Tape
- ○ Pencil or Pen
- ○ Pallet
- ○ Drill and Screws

WHAT TO DO

1   Wrap your hanger tape around one of your terra cotta pots until it overlaps by one or two holes.

2   Cut the hanger tape with your tin snips.

3 Use your first cut piece of hanger tape as a guide to cut additional pieces. Cut a piece for each pot you want to hang.

4 Use your measuring tape and pencil or pen to mark on the pallet where you want to place your pots.

5 Wrap each cut piece of hanger tape into a circle.

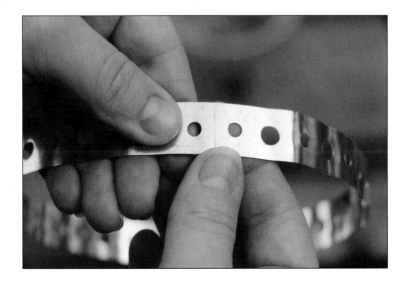

6   Place a screw through the overlapping hole.

7   Screw your hanger tape rings onto the pallet.

8   Place your pots into the hanger tape rings and then plant your succulents, or vice versa.

CARE INSTRUCTIONS

Place your pallet in an area of your garden that receives bright but indirect sunlight and a few hours of direct sunlight throughout the day. You may want to remove your pots when watering to avoid muddy water dripping onto your lower plants.

TIP!
Customize your pallet
garden by painting
your pallet or your
pots.

Chapter 5

Succulent Accessories

Because succulents can survive for extended periods of time as cuttings without soil or water, they make perfect living accessories. Embellish what would be an ordinary hair clip with succulents to create a gorgeous, organic-feeling hairstyle. Wear your favorite plants around your neck or show off your green thumb with a stunning succulent ring. Succulents are perfect natural accessories for use in weddings, since they can be created days, even weeks, in advance.

TERRARIUM NECKLACE

You can bring a miniature living succulent with you wherever you go when you have a terrarium necklace. It's like a delightful little ecosystem around your neck. You can find the type of vial with a hook top in the jewelry section of most craft stores. This necklace makes a lovely gift for anyone who loves to garden.

WHAT YOU NEED

- ○ Glass vial, approximately 2", with hook top
- ○ Necklace Chain of your choice
- ○ Sand
- ○ Activated Charcoal
- ○ Soil
- ○ Moss
- ○ Baby Succulent
- ○ Tweezers
- ○ Pliers

WHAT TO DO

1 Begin by adding four layers to your glass vial. Just as with a full-sized terrarium, these base layers will serve a purpose (assisting with drainage) while adding interest to your necklace. Add your sand, activated charcoal, soil, and moss, in that order.

2 Use your tweezers to slide your plant into the vial. Try to hold your plant by the stem if the opening of the vial is big enough. You will need to wiggle the stem through the moss and into the soil. Make sure to choose a plant that is small enough to fit through the opening, but big enough to make a statement. The tiny succulent should be the focal point of the necklace.

3   Attach your necklace chain to your glass vial. I purchased a vial that already had a ring or "jump chain" attached. All I had to do was use my pliers to open the ring, wrap it around the necklace chain, and then squeeze the ring closed again.

CARE INSTRUCTIONS

Water your baby succulent every couple of days (or when you notice the soil is dry) with a few drops of water. Succulents don't like humidity or sitting in water, so if you notice condensation in your vial, open it up and let it air out. Make sure to keep your necklace out of direct sunlight to avoid burning your baby plant.

SUCCULENT RING

Forget diamonds. Succulents are a girl's best friend! A succulent ring is the perfect accessory to show off your green thumb. This unusual piece will garner compliments wherever you go.

WHAT YOU NEED

- ○ Blank Ring Bezel
- ○ Scissors
- ○ Floral Glue
- ○ Small Succulents

WHAT TO DO

1 Cut the stems off of your plants. Try to cut them as close to the lower leaves as possible while keeping the rosettes intact.

2 Cover the flat surface of your ring bezel with floral glue.

3 Gently press your plants onto your ring bezel.

Your succulents will not be able to survive too long glued to your ring bezel. (Depending on the type of plant, it could last from a few weeks to a month or two.) Once your plants begin to shrivel, carefully remove them and glue on fresh succulents. Floral glue is kind of like rubber cement, so it peels off easily—you should end up with a clean base again. After removing your plants from your ring, gently remove any glue that may be on the lower leaves, place them on top of well-draining soil, and water them occasionally. New roots may sprout if your plant is not damaged too badly by the glue and removal process.

TIP!
Be sure you let your tiny plants callus over for a day or two before gluing them to your ring bezel. This will help your plants absorb less of the glue through the fresh cut, which should help it to last longer.

HEADBAND

People have been wearing flowers in their hair since the beginning of time, so why not try succulents there? Unlike flowers that quickly die, succulents can last weeks, even months, without soil or water, making them a perfect living accessory. Whether for a special occasion like an outdoor wedding or day-to-day wear, succulent hair accessories have an unrivaled natural beauty.

WHAT YOU NEED

- ○ Green Felt
- ○ Scissors
- ○ Headband
- ○ Hot Glue
- ○ Succulent Cuttings

WHAT TO DO

1 Cut two circles out of your felt. You will want the circles to be about the size of your plant or group of plants since it is going to serve as the base or support for them.

2 Decide where you want your plants to sit on the headband and glue one of the circles to the underside of the headband and the other circle on top of it.

3   Make sure your succulent cuttings have their stems cut as close to the base of the plant as possible.

4   Hold your plants upside down, apply hot glue to the lower leaves, and gently press the plants onto the felt circle base that you attached to your headband.

CARE INSTRUCTIONS

When your succulents begin to wither, carefully remove them from your headband and plant them in well-draining soil.

5   Use your scissors to cut away any part of the felt circle that is not hidden by your plants.

TIP!

Headbands not your favorite hair accessory? You can easily create a stunning hair clip by hot-gluing succulents to a blank French clip or barrette.

CROWN

Fresh-flower crowns are lovely, but some flowers are so delicate that the crown is barely usable. Here's a stunning and sturdier alternative: a breathtaking succulent crown! Whether it's your wedding day or you just want to feel like a princess, a succulent crown is sure to make a lasting impression.

WHAT YOU NEED

- ○ Thick Floral Wire (22-gauge)
- ○ Pliers
- ○ Floral Tape
- ○ Succulent Cuttings
- ○ Scissors
- ○ Thin Floral Wire (26-gauge)
- ○ Wire Cutters

WHAT TO DO

1   Use your thicker floral wire to create a circle that fits around your head where you want your crown to sit. Twist the ends of the wire together to close the circle, and then wrap the circle in floral tape.

2   Cut the stems of your plants short with your scissors. Cut a piece of thin wire about 6" long. Insert the thin wire into the stem of each plant.

3   Bend the wire in half.

4 Wrap the stem with the end of the wire to strengthen it and secure it to the wire. Because succulents bruise and scar easily, you will want to be careful not to handle them too roughly during this process.

5 Once you've got several succulents stemmed with the thin wire, choose a plant to attach first. Place it on the wire circle where you want it and wrap its wire around the circle. You can use your pliers to squeeze the wires tightly together and to pinch down the ends.

6 Continue choosing plants, placing them on the wire where you like, until your circle is full of beautiful plants. I decided to only do the front half of my crown, but you can do the entire thing if you want. If you have exposed wires, wrap the back half in floral tape once more.

Although the succulents on your crown are still alive, it is not technically a "living" succulent crown in that the plants will eventually die if left attached to the wire. Depending on the type of plants you used, this could take a couple of weeks to a month or so. You will definitely get a lot more use out of your succulent crown than you would a fresh-flower crown. If you would like to keep your plants alive, remove them from the wire once they begin to wither, let the stems callus over for a few days, and plant them in well-draining soil.

TIP!
Adding a few succulents in a contrasting shade like purple adds visual interest to the crown.

Photo credit: Tayia Rae Photography

LIVING NECKLACE

Here's another accessory option that's easy to make but looks stunning. Not only are the baby succulents absolutely adorable, but people will be astonished when they realize you are wearing living plants around your neck!

WHAT YOU NEED

- ○ Scissors
- ○ Necklace Cord or Chain
- ○ Pendant Bezel, approximately 1¼"
- ○ Floral Glue
- ○ Moss
- ○ Pencil or similar pointy tool
- ○ Baby Succulents

WHAT TO DO

1 Use your scissors to cut the stems of your baby plants a little shorter than the depth of your bezel.

2 Coat the inside of your bezel with floral glue and press in your moss. Allow a few minutes to dry.

3 Use a pencil or other pointy tool to create a little hole in the moss where you will place the stem of your first succulent.

4 Carefully hold your baby plant, stem facing up. Squeeze your floral glue onto the lower leaves of the plant, taking care not to cover the stem with glue, as this is where roots will eventually sprout from.

5 Decide where to place your plant and gently press it into the moss. Repeat steps 3, 4, and 5 until you have placed all of your desired plants into your bezel.

6 Attach a necklace cord or chain to your bezel.

CARE INSTRUCTIONS

Mist the moss every few days to encourage roots to form on the stems of your plants. Your necklace should last anywhere from a few weeks to a few months, depending on the types of plants you choose. Certain succulents may be more sensitive to the floral glue and will not root. If your plant does not start to root, simply remove it when it begins to wither and replace it with a new plant.

Chapter 6

Succulent Holidays

It's always exciting to change up your home decor throughout the seasons to coincide with different holidays. Whether you like to go all out or just add a few touches here and there, you can easily incorporate succulents into your holiday decor no matter what time of year it is. In this chapter, we will create six gorgeous succulent projects that will breathe new life into your seasonal favorites. From stunning succulent-topped pumpkins to adorable succulent-filled Easter eggs, you're sure to fall in love with these charming new traditions.

SUCCULENT-TOPPED PUMPKIN

Succulent-topped pumpkins are a rising trend in fall decor and it's no wonder why! Succulents come in a variety of colors that look stunning paired with pumpkins of all shapes and sizes. A succulent-topped pumpkin makes an eye-catching centerpiece at an autumn gathering or a perfect accessory for your front porch.

- Pumpkin
- Floral Glue or Hot Glue
- Sphagnum Moss
- Succulent or Succulent Cuttings
- Scissors

WHAT TO DO

1 Snap the stem off your pumpkin. Pumpkin stems usually pop right off, but if yours is troublesome, you can saw it off.

2 Apply floral or hot glue to the top of your pumpkin.

3   Press your moss onto the glue.

4   Hold your plant upside down and apply floral or hot glue to the lower leaves.

5   Carefully press your plant onto the moss. Repeat steps 4 and 5 if you are using multiple plants.

6   Cut off any sphagnum moss that is out of place.

CARE INSTRUCTIONS

Keep your succulent-topped pumpkin out of direct sunlight. Wet moss thoroughly about once a week. Since the pumpkins are not cut, this project will last months with proper care. When the pumpkin does begin to rot, though, carefully remove your succulents and plant them in well-draining soil.

TIP!
You can also cut the top off of your pumpkin, scoop out the insides, add soil, and plant whole succulents directly into your pumpkin. Since carved pumpkins rot more quickly, this technique will not last as long as the gluing method.

TOPIARY BALL

Throughout the year, you may notice a lot of stores carry faux topiary balls to coincide with the different holidays. It's easy to breathe new life into these artificial topiaries by attaching real succulents to them. You can add different colors, styles, or sizes of plants to take the faux arrangement up a notch. Topiary balls are fantastic year-round!

WHAT YOU NEED

- ○ Succulent Cuttings
- ○ Floral Wire (22-gauge)
- ○ Floral Tape
- ○ Faux Topiary Ball (with foam center)

WHAT TO DO

1 Wrap the stems of your succulent cuttings with floral wire and leave a couple of inches of wire at the end. I've listed 22-gauge floral wire in the materials list, but use something thicker if the stems of your plants are thicker or if your foam ball is hard to penetrate.

2 Wrap the succulent stems with floral tape. Start as close to the base of your plant as possible and wrap until you get to the end of the stem of your plant.

3 Hold your cutting by the stem and insert the tip of the wire into the foam center of your topiary ball. If your succulent sticks out too far, cut the wire shorter and reinsert it into the foam ball. Make sure to sprinkle your succulents evenly throughout the topiary ball.

CARE INSTRUCTIONS

Keep your topiary out of harsh direct sunlight. When your plants begin to wither, remove them from the topiary, remove the floral tape and wire, and plant them in well-draining soil.

GLASS BULB ORNAMENT

Give your Christmas tree a modern flair with a gorgeous air plant–filled glass bulb ornament. (See Chapter 1 for more information on air plants.) Since air plants do not require soil to survive, your ornament has a clean and stunning simplicity.

WHAT YOU NEED

- ○ Hanging Glass Bulb Terrarium
- ○ White Sand
- ○ Air Plant
- ○ Faux Holly Berries

WHAT TO DO

1   Pour a thin layer of white sand in the bottom of your glass bulb. The sand is decorative and reminiscent of snow!

2   Insert your air plant into the bulb. It can rest on top of the sand. Let some of the plant hang out of the opening if you like the look.

3   Add some faux holly berries for a pop of color.

CARE INSTRUCTIONS

Place your bulb where it will get plenty of bright indirect sunlight. You should remove your air plant about once per week to water it. You can water by rinsing it under running water, or let the entire plant soak in water for about 20 minutes. Let it dry for a few hours before replacing it in the glass bulb.

TIP!

You can also create a traditional succulent terrarium in a hanging glass bulb!

See "Succulent Terrarium" project in Chapter 3 for more information. Place the terrarium in indirect sunlight. Glass magnifies light and heat, so be careful not to place your terrarium where it will receive a lot of direct sunlight. Stick a finger down into the soil to be sure the soil is completely dry before each watering.

LIVING CHRISTMAS TREE

A living succulent Christmas tree is a fabulous way to enhance your home for the holidays. Its striking beauty and low maintenance make it an innovative alternative to a traditional Christmas tree. If you are eco-conscious or just love the look of these gorgeous arrangements, a succulent Christmas tree is sure to be your favorite holiday decor tradition for years to come.

WHAT YOU NEED

- ○ Posterboard or Paper
- ○ Two Pencils
- ○ String
- ○ Scissors
- ○ Hardware Cloth or Chicken Wire
- ○ Wire Cutters
- ○ Tape
- ○ Yardstick or Measuring Tape
- ○ Floral Wire
- ○ Sphagnum Moss
- ○ Succulent Cuttings
- ○ Floral Pins

WHAT TO DO

1 Start by creating a circle template out of paper. Depending on how big you want to make your Christmas tree, you may need to use posterboard or tape some pieces of paper together. I used a 24" × 10' piece of silver galvanized steel hardware cloth, so the biggest circle I could make had a 2' diameter.

> **TIP!**
> If you want to make a smaller tree, you can use a pan lid, wreath frame, or other circular item as your template. This will save you time, eliminating the first few steps of this project.

2 Tie your pencils together with string to create a makeshift compass.

3 Hold one pencil in the center of your paper and draw a circle with the other pencil.

4 Cut out your circle.

5 Roll out your piece of chicken wire or hardware cloth (you can find these at your local home center) and place your paper circle on top of it. If your circle is large you can stand on your paper, or tape it to the wire to hold it in place. (You may want to wear gloves when working with hardware cloth or chicken wire.)

6 Use wire cutters to cut the circle out of your wire or cloth following the template you made.

7 Now you will need to cut a triangle or "slice" out of your wire circle to create a cone. It should look like you removed one slice from a pie. The bigger the slice you remove, the smaller the base of your cone will be. You can try to measure your angle with a yardstick or measuring tape but it's hard to draw on wire and also difficult to cut a straight line. I used a measuring tape to find the exact center of my wire circle and then began cutting one side of my slice. I cut one vertical wire, moved down a square, cut another vertical wire, moved to the left one square, and cut a horizontal wire. Repeat this pattern until you get to the outer edge of the circle. Go back to the center of the circle and repeat the cutting pattern in reverse to create the other side of your slice.

8 Now that you have removed the slice from your circle (which should now resemble Pac-Man), you can roll your wire into a cone shape. Depending on the thickness of your wire, this may be more difficult than it sounds. You may need to overlap the sides to create a flat surface for your cone to stand on.

9 Once you have rolled your cone into the desired form, secure it into place with floral wire.

10 Turn the cone upside down and fill it with dampened sphagnum moss.

11 If your sphagnum moss wants to fall out of the bottom of your tree, you can use your floral wire to create a barrier across the opening of the cone.

12 Stand your cone up on a flat surface, point up, like a Christmas tree.

13 Begin planting your succulent cuttings in the tree. If you find it difficult to insert your stems into the moss, use a pencil or other pointy tool to create holes in which to push your stems.

14 Use larger plants toward the bottom of your tree and small cuttings toward the top. You can create a pattern with your plants or just insert them randomly. I like the way a swirl pattern grabs your attention and draws your eye around the tree.

15 If your cuttings have short stems or just don't want to stay on the tree, you can fasten them into place with floral pins.

CARE INSTRUCTIONS

Place your tree in bright, indirect sunlight. Water when the sphagnum moss becomes dry. Be sure to rotate your tree occasionally to allow even sun exposure.

14

TIP!
To create a larger tree, try wrapping a tapered tomato cage with chicken wire to serve as your frame!

EGG CRATE

Nothing says "Happy Easter" like a crate full of colorful pastel eggs! For a special twist, though, add baby succulents to your Easter decor. Filling an egg crate with succulent-filled eggs creates a perfect springtime centerpiece that you'll want to keep around long after Easter has come and gone.

WHAT YOU NEED

- Eggs
- Succulent Soil
- Baby Succulents
- Egg Crate
- Moss (Optional)
- Faux Flowers (Optional)

WHAT TO DO

1 Gently crack your eggs near the top and save or discard the egg whites and yolks.

2 Rinse the eggs out with water and let dry.

3 Fill your eggshells with succulent soil. Lightly pack in the soil all the way to the top.

4 Plant your baby succulents in your eggshells. You can plant one larger succulent or a few little ones in each shell.

5 Create a complete arrangement by placing your succulent-filled eggshells into your egg crate. Create interest by leaving some slots empty or by planting a succulent directly into the egg crate.

6 Add moss to empty slots in your crate or around plants to add color and texture to your arrangement.

7 If you like the look, add a couple of faux flowers to enhance the springtime feel.

CARE INSTRUCTIONS

Place your succulent-filled egg crate in bright, indirect sunlight and water when the soil is completely dry.

TIP!
Use a ceramic egg crate if you intend on planting succulents directly into the crate. Paper cartons will become weak over time as you water your plants and will leak.

EASTER BASKET WREATH

A lot of Easter decor tends to be over the top when it comes to bright colors, plastic eggs, and gigantic bows. If you are looking for something a little more subtle with a natural, earthy feel, this Easter wreath will be right up your alley.

WHAT YOU NEED

○ Eggs
○ Oval Grapevine Wreath with Basket Bottom
○ Sphagnum Moss
○ Succulents
○ Faux Flowers

WHAT TO DO

1 Gently crack your eggs near the top and save or discard the egg whites and yolks.

2 Rinse the eggs out with water and let dry.

3 Fill the basket of your wreath with sphagnum moss.

4 Arrange your eggs where you want them in the basket, with their intact ends up. I used colorful eggs from my neighbor's chickens, but you can use white or brown eggs from the store.

5 Plant your succulents in the sphagnum moss. I tried to use plants that matched my eggs and had a pastel, springtime feel!

6 Stick faux flowers into the wreath for a finishing touch.

CARE INSTRUCTIONS

Hang your wreath where it will not receive a lot of harsh direct sunlight. Water when the sphagnum moss becomes dry.

TIP!
Grapevine wreaths come in many shapes and sizes and can be used for a variety of holidays! Don't limit yourself to only using this wreath for Easter. You can change out your plants and decor throughout the year to complement every season.

Chapter 7

Celebrating with Succulents

Succulents are a stylish way to bring a natural element to your special day. They can be used in almost every aspect of a wedding, dinner party, or baby or bridal shower—from boutonnieres and bouquets to centerpieces and party favors. Whether you are hosting a modern or rustic affair, succulents can fit the theme—they can have either a classic or a contemporary feel, depending on how you arrange them. Pair them with traditional floral arrangements to create arrays of unrivaled beauty. Perhaps the best part? Unlike conventional flowers, succulents can be planted after your event, and with proper care will last for years to come, serving as a treasured keepsake.

PLACECARD HOLDER

Your guests will be delighted when they find their seat held by this charming little potted succulent. This succulent placecard holder can also double as a party favor, giving you more bang for your buck!

WHAT YOU NEED

- ○ Small Terra Cotta Pots
- ○ Succulent Soil
- ○ Succulents
- ○ Moss
- ○ Pen
- ○ Paper Flags attached to Sticks

WHAT TO DO

1. Fill your terra cotta pots ¾ full with succulent soil and plant your succulents.

2. Cover the soil in your pots with moss to create a finished look.

3. Write your guests' names on your paper flags and insert the sticks into the soil on the side of each pot. (I bought the paper flags already assembled at a craft store.)

CARE INSTRUCTIONS

Your potted succulent placecard holders should be kept in bright, indirect sunlight. Water when the soil is completely dry.

> **TIP!**
> Paint your pots or tie a bow around them with ribbon or twine to customize their look to fit the style of your event. You can also make printed labels on your home printer if you'd like a more finished look for your text. Give guests succulent care instructions on the back of the label.

BABY FOOD JAR
PARTY FAVOR

Not only are baby food jars adorably small, but they are readily available and inexpensive. If you have a baby yourself, or know someone who does, chances are you can get a lot of jars for free. Your guests will fall in love with their new mini garden, and you can feel great about giving them a charming upcycled gift! These work great as favors for weddings, baby showers, or even small dinner parties.

WHAT YOU NEED

- ○ Baby Food Jars
- ○ Pebbles
- ○ Succulent Soil
- ○ Pencil or similar pointy tool
- ○ Small Succulents
- ○ Pen
- ○ Favor Tags
- ○ Thin Twine

WHAT TO DO

1 Line the bottom of your baby food jars with a layer of pebbles to create an alternative drainage system.

2 Fill the rest of your jars with well-draining soil.

3 Plant your succulents. If it's easier, use a pencil or similar pointy tool to create a hole in the soil where you want to plant your succulent. You can plant one succulent or a few smaller ones.

4 Use your pen to write "Thank You" on your favor tags.

5 Attach the favor tags to your baby food jars with the thin twine. You can tie the ends in a bow or knot, depending on your preference.

CARE INSTRUCTIONS

Since baby food jars do not have proper drainage holes, you will need to water these mini arrangements less often than your other plants. Succulents don't do well when their roots are sitting in soggy soil, so take special care to only water your jars when the soil is completely dry.

TIP!
This project can double as a placecard holder! Instead of writing "Thank You" on the tag, you can write your guests' names and leave the little favor on their place setting.

NAPKIN RING

Napkin rings are a small accessory that can make a huge statement on your tablescape. Using living plants on your napkin rings adds a touch of natural elegance that faux plants just can't match. These are perfect in an outdoor or porch setting. Baby's breath or wax flowers make dainty fillers to use along with your succulents.

WHAT YOU NEED

- ○ Floral Wire
- ○ Wire Cutters
- ○ Floral Tape
- ○ Succulent Cuttings
- ○ Flowers

WHAT TO DO

1 Create a ring out of floral wire. You can wrap it in floral tape if you wish to create a thicker ring.

2 Group together your succulents and flowers into a little bouquet. Wrap the stems together with floral wire.

3   Attach the bouquet to your ring with floral tape. If your plants are heavy, you may want to attach them to the ring with floral wire followed by floral tape.

CARE INSTRUCTIONS

When your event is over, dismantle your napkin rings and plant your succulents in well-draining soil. With proper care, your succulents will continue to thrive!

CENTERPIECE

When creating centerpieces for an event, you usually want to keep the cost to a minimum since you will be making at least one for each table. Rather than spending a fortune on fancy logs from a craft store, or chopping down trees yourself, this project repurposes wood from an unlikely and inexpensive source: lawn edging! Rustic logs paired with stunning gold-painted succulents will bring a charming simplicity and elegance to your special day.

WHAT YOU NEED

- ○ Wooden Lawn Edging Logs
- ○ Scissors or Razor Blade
- ○ Lace or Burlap
- ○ Hot Glue
- ○ Succulents
- ○ Gold Spray Paint, or other color
- ○ Flowers

WHAT TO DO

1 Wooden lawn edging comes attached together by a thin plastic strip. Use your scissors or a razor blade to cut apart your logs.

2 Hot-glue a strip of lace or burlap around the bottom of three of the logs to cover where you cut the plastic. You can make the strip whatever width you'd like.

3 Hot-glue the three logs together. If you don't want to hold them together while the glue sets, tie them together with a string and let them sit until the glue has completely dried.

4 There will be a hole in the center where the three logs meet. You can use this hole as a "vase" for flower stems. (Keep in mind that you're not using soil or water, so you'll need to find plants that won't need water or use faux flowers.)

5   Choose a succulent or a couple of them, cut off their stems, and spray-paint them gold or another color that fits with the color palette of your event.

6   Place your spray-painted succulent on top of your logs along with some flowers of your choice.

CARE INSTRUCTIONS

When your event is over, plant your succulents in well-draining soil. With proper care, even your spray-painted succulents will continue to thrive!

BOUTONNIERE

Boutonnieres are commonly worn by men at weddings and other special occasions. At weddings, boutonnieres traditionally complement the bride's bouquet. They are very simple to make, and if they are made entirely of succulents they can be assembled days, even weeks, in advance.

WHAT YOU NEED

- ○ Succulent Cutting
- ○ Flowers
- ○ Floral Wire
- ○ Wire Cutters
- ○ Green Floral Tape
- ○ Jute Twine (Optional)
- ○ Boutonniere Pin

WHAT TO DO

1   If your succulent does not have a very long stem (shorter than an inch), you will need to stem your plant. Insert floral wire into the short stem of your succulent. Cut the wire to the length you want your stem to be. Wrap the plant's stem with floral tape. Begin as close to the base of the plant as possible and work your way down to the end of the wire.

2   Group together your succulent with one or two other flowers, or greenery. I used blue thistle and wax flower. The succulent should be the focal point.

3   Wrap the group of stems with floral wire followed by floral tape. Add a boutonniere pin to attach the arrangement to a suit or shirt.

CARE INSTRUCTIONS

When your event is over, dismantle your boutonniere and de-stem your succulent cutting by removing the floral wire. Let it callus over for a few days and then plant it in well-draining soil. With proper care, your succulent will continue to thrive!

TIP!
To create a more natural look, wrap the stems in jute twine after the floral tape.

BOUQUET

It's no surprise that succulents are being used more and more in weddings and other special events. Because they come in a variety of colors, shapes, and sizes, succulents can fit into any style bouquet. Whether you want your bouquet completely made of succulents, or prefer to use them alongside other flowers, they are sure to make a statement. In addition to being an absolutely gorgeous addition to your wedding, your succulents can be replanted and last long after your event is over, making a perfect keepsake from your special day.

WHAT YOU NEED

- ○ Succulents
- ○ Green Floral Stem Wire or Skewers (approximately 12")
- ○ Green Floral Wire
- ○ Wire Cutters
- ○ Floral Tape
- ○ Flowers
- ○ Lace, Burlap, or Ribbon
- ○ Scissors
- ○ Hot Glue or Boutonniere Pins

WHAT TO DO

1   Remove all of the soil from your succulents. If your succulents have long roots, you may want to trim them or simply cut the roots off leaving a one- or two-inch stem.

2   Insert your floral stem wire or skewer into the stem of your succulent. A skewer is my first choice for large plants, because it provides a very sturdy support for the weight of heavy succulents. If your succulent has a thin stem, I recommend using floral wire to avoid tearing open the stem with a thick skewer. Using floral wire also gives you a little more freedom to angle your plants as you build your bouquet.

3   Wrap the stem of your plant with floral tape. Start as close to the base of the plant as possible and work your way down the wire or skewer.

4   Wrap all the way to the end of the skewer if you want all of the stems in your bouquet to be green.

5   If you have a succulent with a short or flimsy stem, or no stem (only roots), you can create support for your plant by wrapping the roots around a skewer and then wrapping them tightly with floral wire followed by floral tape.

6   After you have stemmed all of your succulents, you are ready to start building your bouquet. Start with one plant or a small grouping as your center and add from there.

7   Use filler flowers, like baby's breath, to add mass to your bouquet. Place taller flowers or clippings to the sides and back of your bouquet.

8   Hold your stems tightly and wrap them together with your lace, burlap, ribbon, or floral tape. Hot-glue the end or use boutonniere pins to secure it into place.

CARE INSTRUCTIONS

Treat your succulent bouquet as you would a flower bouquet. When your event is over, dismantle your bouquet and de-stem your succulents. Let them callus over for a few days and then plant them in well-draining soil. With proper care, this special keepsake will continue to thrive.

TIP!

Take special care when handling your succulents. Many succulent leaves have a beautiful coating that can be rubbed off if touched. Try to hold your plants by the stems or under the lower leaves as much as possible to keep them looking their best.

About the Author

TAWNI DAIGLE lives with her husband and four children in sunny San Diego, California. She is passionate about growing and propagating succulents and enjoys sharing her knowledge with others through her blog, *Needles + Leaves* (*http://needlesandleaves.net*), where she shares DIY tutorials, garden tours, home decor style features, and more.

Index

Note: Page numbers in *italics* indicate projects.

T

V

W